Inventing Oatmeal

by Christian Downey
illustrated by Victor Kennedy

Editorial Offices: Glenview, Illinois • Parsippany, New Jersey • New York, New York
Sales Offices: Needham, Massachusetts • Duluth, Georgia • Glenview, Illinois
Coppell, Texas • Ontario, California • Mesa, Arizona

Every effort has been made to secure permission and provide appropriate credit for photographic material. The publisher deeply regrets any omission and pledges to correct errors called to its attention in subsequent editions.

Unless otherwise acknowledged, all photographs are the property of Scott Foresman, a division of Pearson Education.

16 ©Firefly Productions/CORBIS

ISBN: 0-328-13463-5

Copyright © Pearson Education, Inc.

All Rights Reserved. Printed in the United States of America. This publication is protected by Copyright, and permission should be obtained from the publisher prior to any prohibited reproduction, storage in a retrieval system, or transmission in any form by any means, electronic, mechanical, photocopying, recording, or likewise. For information regarding permission(s), write to: Permissions Department, Scott Foresman, 1900 East Lake Avenue, Glenview, Illinois 60025.

7 8 9 10 V0G1 14 13 12 11 10 09 08

On the weekends, Grace and her brother Ben liked to play in the garage. Their father moved his car so they could set up a science table. Their mother often helped them work on fun projects.

One day, Grace and Ben decided to try out their new chemistry set. It was a gift from Aunt Amy. She was a scientist herself.

They set up their table and got to work. They had borrowed things from the kitchen to test out their new set. There was a glass of milk, some cereal flakes, and a glass of juice. "Let's pour the milk into the test tube," said Grace.

"Pour in the juice too," said Ben. "And the cereal flakes."

"It looks like soup!" laughed Grace. She furiously stirred the mixture with a long straw.

Grace and Ben stepped back and looked at what they had made. The mixture in the test tube was thick and white.

"Eww! What is it?" asked Grace.

"I think we invented oatmeal!" said Ben.

"Oatmeal already exists! We didn't invent it," said Grace.

"We invented cold oatmeal!" Ben said. "Did you know in England people call it porridge? I did. I'm a genius."

"I don't think geniuses are so messy," laughed Grace. Ben had spilled the thick white mixture all down his shirt.

"Did they always call it porridge?" asked Grace.

"Ever since the Middle Ages," said Ben.

"Wouldn't it be fun to have lived back then?" Grace asked. "I wish we could invent a time machine and see how people lived."

"Who needs a time machine?" asked Ben. "We have our imagination! We can pretend we're kids living during the Middle Ages!"

Grace closed her eyes. Ben closed his eyes too. "Picture us inside a castle," he said. "We're not in the garage anymore. We're not even in the United States. When you open your eyes, we will be in England during the Middle Ages!"

Slowly, they each opened their eyes.

Grace couldn't believe her eyes. She looked at the red velvet curtains and huge stone walls. She was in a real castle! "Ben, it worked!" she cried.

Ben poked his head around the heavy curtain. "I told you we could imagine this!"

"Do you think there's a princess here? With long, golden braids?" asked Grace.

"That's a fairy tale!" said Ben. "I want to find the dungeon where they keep the criminals! Let's go!"

Before they could go anywhere, they heard the sound of footsteps coming closer. Grace and Ben hid behind the curtains. They peeked out and saw a well-dressed young man walk into the room. A short man wearing dirty clothes was with him.

"My lord, oh noble one," said the short man. "Do you think her majesty would enjoy beets and turnips from the garden? I could bring her some!"

"That would be nice," said the young man.

"Anything to repay you for keeping us safe," smiled the short man.

Ben and Grace came out of hiding. "I bet that guy in the nice clothes was a duke," Ben said. "That's a kind of ruler. The short man was a poor peasant. Peasants lived on land owned by rich people. They work for the duke, who protects them."

"Who protects the duke?" asked Grace.

"The king and queen!" said Ben. "Let's go find them!"

Grace and Ben explored the castle. Ben found the dungeon, which was a cold basement, but it was empty. Grace liked the long dining room full of candles. Ben liked the suit of armor he found. After an hour or so, they found themselves outside a kitchen. "I hear voices," Grace whispered. They hid by the door to listen.

12

"I wish her majesty would have something new for supper," sighed a female voice. "She only eats porridge! Porridge, porridge, porridge! I'm a cook who only makes porridge!"

Grace and Ben made a face. "Nothing but porridge? Eww!" said Grace. "I don't want to stay here! Let's imagine ourselves back home!"

Grace and Ben shut their eyes tightly and thought of home. Nothing happened! Hearing footsteps again, Grace and Ben hid as well as they could. The duke and duchess would be going to the dining room for their porridge any second. "Think harder!" Grace whispered.

Suddenly, everything grew quiet. Slowly, Grace and Ben opened their eyes again. They were back in their own garage!

"It worked, Ben!" said Grace.

"See, Grace? We don't need a time machine to travel," said Ben.

Just then, their mother walked into the garage. "It's time for dinner!" she said.

"What's for dinner, Mom?" asked Grace.

"Anything but porridge, please!" said Ben. He and Grace laughed and laughed as they followed their mother into the house.

Early Chemistry

What we now know as chemistry used to be called *alchemy.* In the Middle Ages scientists were called *alchemists.* Alchemists tried to turn lead into gold. This discovery would have made the scientists rich! However, no alchemist ever figured out how to do it. Alchemists were very private. Their writings were often in code so that others could not understand them. But as they experimented and learned, alchemists paved the way for modern day chemistry.